The Ultimate Motorcycles

SPORT BIKES

<u>Lori Kinstad Pupeza</u>
ABDO Publishing Company

visit us at
www.abdopub.com

Published by Abdo Publishing Company 4940 Viking Drive, Edina, Minnesota 55435. Copyright © 1998 by Abdo Consulting Group, Inc. International copyrights reserved in all countries. No part of this book may be reproduced in any form without written permission from the publisher.

Printed in the United States.

Photo credits: Allsport, Duomo, Peter Arnold, Inc., Sportschrome, SuperStock

Edited by Kal Gronvall

Library of Congress Cataloging-in-Publication Data

Pupeza, Lori Kinstad
     Sport bikes / Lori Kinstad Pupeza.
          p.   cm. -- (The ultimate motorcycle series)
     Includes index.
     Summary: Discusses the development of the motorcycle with emphasis on sport bikes, the biggest and most powerful motorcycles made.
       ISBN 1-57765-004-2
     1. Motorcycles--Juvenile literature.   2. Motorcycles, Racing--Juvenile literature
     [1.Motorcycles.] I. Title. II. Series: Pupeza, Lori Kinstad. Ultimate motorcycle series
     TL440.15.P875 1998
     629.227'5--dc21
                                                                97-53091
                                                                CIP
                                                                AC

Warning: The series *The Ultimate Motorcycles* is intended as entertainment for children. These activities should never be attempted without training, instruction, supervision, and proper equipment.

Contents

On the Road

Sport bikes are built for speed. They are the biggest and most powerful motorcycles made. Today, people drive them everywhere, whizzing through traffic or racing them on a track. Some sport bikes that are made for drag racing can go over 200 miles per hour (322 kmph)! Until the 1950s, most motorcycles were built by the British, Italians, Germans, or Americans. When the Japanese came out with their version of the motorcycle, two wheeled transportation took on a totally new meaning. Honda was the first Japanese company to build a sport bike. Since then, sport bikes have become popular because of their sporty look and fun, quick handling.

Opposite page: Many people ride sport bikes for the speed.

The Early Years of Two-Wheeled Transportation

The motorcycle started out as just a bicycle with an engine attached to it. Two French brothers, Ernest and Pierre Michaux, along with the help of Louis Guillaume Perreaux, put together the first motorized bicycle. They attached a small steam engine to a bicycle. The unstable bike was nicknamed the "bone shaker." A belt connected the engine to the back wheel of the bike.

The invention was not very powerful, but the bike did make it about 10 miles (16 km) to a neighboring town. The driver had a hot ride because he had to sit right on top of the engine's boiler.

The invention was a hit all over the world. In New York there was even a "Michaux Club," honoring one of the inventors. At the same time that the Michaux brothers and Perreaux were working on their motorcycle, an American named Sylvester Roper was building a similar motorized two-wheeler. But because his patents had no dates, he wasn't given credit for being the first to build a motorcycle.

Others tried to improve the steam-driven motorcycle, but nothing worked quite as well for a power source as the internal combustion engine. In 1876, a German engineer named Nikolaus

Otto built the first internal combustion engine. It was called an internal combustion engine because fuel was burned inside the engine. This led to the first gasoline-driven motorcycle. In 1885, two Germans, Gottlieb Daimler and Wilhelm Maybach, put a similar engine onto a wooden frame. Daimler's son, 17 year old Paul, rode this motorcycle for 10 miles (16 km). During the ride, the seat caught on fire because it was too close to the hot engine!

This 1949 NSU Fox is an early relative to the modern motorcycle.

The Motorcycle Goes into Production

Only nine years after that disaster happened, Daimler and Maybach became partners with Alois Wolfmuller in order to build a motorcycle that they could sell to the public. They built a twin-cylinder motorcycle. They sold over 1,000 motorcycles in the first two years of production. But they didn't turn out to be very reliable machines. People stopped buying them, and production ended in 1897.

Early bike designers couldn't find the right place to put the engine. Some put the engine at the rear, with a bar attached to the seat. Others put the engine on a trolley, which the motorcycle pulled behind on a third wheel. In 1901, the first mass-produced motorcycle had its engine between the wheels. It was called the Werner bike. By this time, motorcycles were being made that could go up to 90 mph (145 kmph). There were many different small companies making motorcycles. Motorcycles were a new invention, and everyone wanted to try to come up with the best design before anybody else did.

Many different makes and models were produced during the first few decades of the motorcycle's birth. In America alone, over 30 makes of motorcycles were being built by 1914. At this time,

Indian was the biggest producer of bikes in the world. The V-twin
engine was the most popular in American
bikes. Harley-Davidson and Excelsior also
used this engine design. At the turn of
the century, motorcyclists needed sturdy,
reliable transportation that could withstand
the vast, rugged lands of America. So
motorcycle companies made solid, yet very
simple machines. The nostalgic feel of the
big American road bike is still alive today,
especially in the Harley-Davidson models.

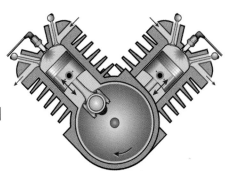

*The V-twin engine is
simply 2 four-stroke
cylinders working
together.*

In America, the Henderson, the Indian, the Excelsior (built by
Schwinn), and the Harley-Davidson were becoming more and more
popular. Germany was known the best for its BMWs. In Great Britain,
the BSA, the Norton, and the Triumph were making a name for
themselves. Lawrence of Arabia owned eight of the British-made
Brough-Superiors (called the Rolls Royce of motorcycles). He died in
a crash while riding one. Italy made the classy Moto Guzzi, the
Benelli, the Ducati, and many
different kinds of scooters.
France, Austria, Czechoslovakia,
Scandinavia, and Spain also had
models of their own.

*Newer Japanese sport bikes look
nothing like the early American and
European motorcycles.*

The Japanese Join the Race

Until the 1950s, most of the motorcycles were made by the British, Italians, Germans, and Americans. About that time, the Japanese decided to join the motorcycle mania going on all over the world. By 1955, Honda was the top motorcycle maker in Japan. Kawasaki, Yamaha, and Suzuki also built similar machines. With the introduction of Japanese bike producers, there came about a technical war to see who could make the fastest, largest, and most mechanically complex machine. In 1969, Honda came out with the CB750, the first sport bike. It was a four-cylinder, five-speed bike with electric start and disc brakes. The CB750 established standards for all sport bikes seen on the roads today. Since then, Japanese motorcycles have swamped the market because they are very reliable and affordable.

Opposite page: The Japanese have become the world leaders in sport bike production with motorcycles such as this Yamaha.

Where They Ride

Many people own sport bikes just to drive around town. Although they aren't the most comfortable motorcycle to ride for long distances, they are good for short rides or for commuting. Sport bikes are built for speed, so the race track is where they can be pushed to their full potential. They are made for smooth handling and leaning through corners.

The first motorcycle race probably took place when two motorcycle enthusiasts first met. There always will be a competitive spirit between motorcyclists, and the race is always about whose motorcycle is faster and more reliable. Avid cyclists have raced motorcycles through deserts, snow, ice, dirt, mud, and custom-built tracks. In fact, motorcycle racing became so popular that the super bike was developed just for that purpose.

Superbike racing started in the United States, but now it's all over the world. Superbikes look like street bikes, but many parts are refined and enhanced for better handling, making a lighter, faster bike. Cycle companies compete with each other to produce the best motorcycle possible for both the racer and the consumer. One of the most famous superbike races is held in Florida, called the Daytona 200. Racers drive for 200 miles (322 km) around the banked track at speeds that exceed 100 mph (161 kmph).

Grand Prix racing has been around since 1913, when France held the first race. Later, that name was given to any famous race. Grand Prix races have been held all over the world. The motorcycles that are raced in the Grand Prix are as high tech as the manufacturer can make them. Years after they were tested on the race track, these new high-tech machines found themselves onto showroom floors.

There are different classes of motorcycles, which are based on engine size. The classes go from 125cc to 750cc engines. The term cc means cubic centimeter. The number indicates the size of the engine. The 500cc class is the most popular.

All types of races, from 125cc to 700cc, are held on a race track. Bikes are outfitted with wide racing slicks that hug the road surface. Racers speed around the track and aggressively try to get ahead before the next turn. Motorcycles in these races are built for top performance. Drivers have to learn how to corner and maneuver the heavy, speeding machines without losing control. These motorcycles weigh around 300 or 400 pounds (136 or 181 kg) and some can go up to speeds of 200 mph (322 kmph).

The Parts of a Sport Bike

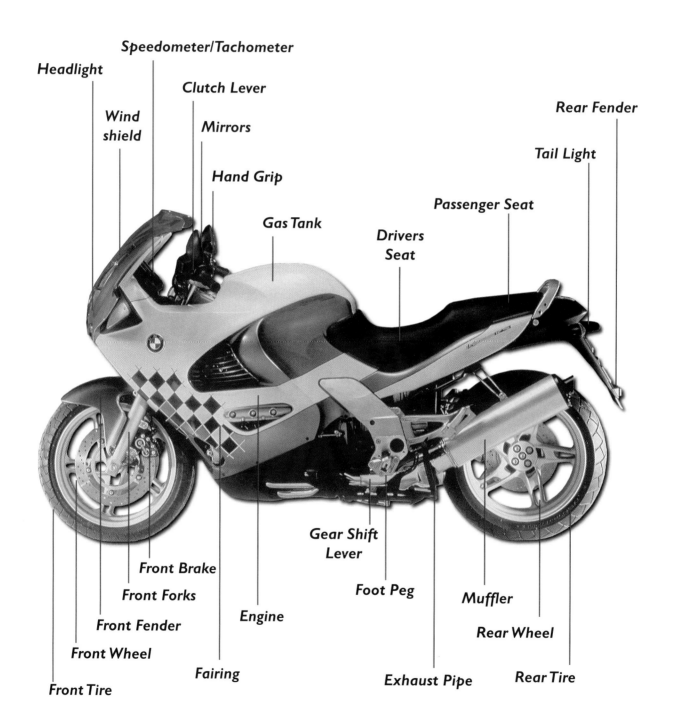

Speedometer/Tachometer

Headlight

Clutch Lever

Rear Fender

Wind shield

Mirrors

Tail Light

Hand Grip

Passenger Seat

Gas Tank

Drivers Seat

Gear Shift Lever

Front Brake

Foot Peg

Front Forks

Muffler

Front Fender

Engine

Rear Wheel

Front Wheel

Fairing

Exhaust Pipe

Rear Tire

Front Tire

How a Four-Stroke Engine Works

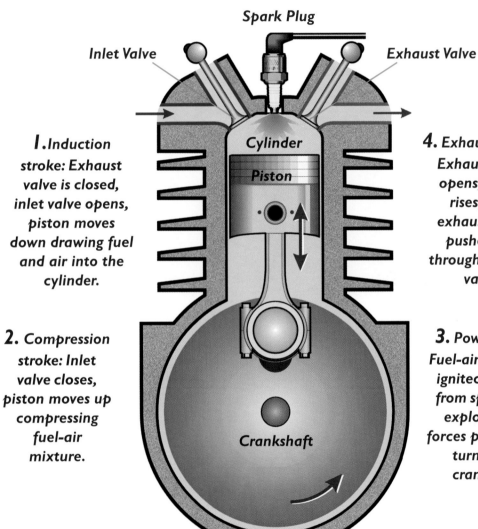

Spark Plug

Inlet Valve

Exhaust Valve

Cylinder

Piston

Crankshaft

1. Induction stroke: Exhaust valve is closed, inlet valve opens, piston moves down drawing fuel and air into the cylinder.

2. Compression stroke: Inlet valve closes, piston moves up compressing fuel-air mixture.

4. Exhaust stroke: Exhaust valve opens, piston rises, used exhaust gas is pushed out through exhaust valve.

3. Power stroke: Fuel-air mixture is ignited by spark from spark plug, exploding gas forces piston down turning the crankshaft.

From the Driver's Seat

Sport bikes are streamlined. That means that exterior parts of the motorcycle are built to be aerodynamic, therefore making the bike go faster. The handlebars are bent downwards, so the driver is leaning forward, creating less wind resistance. The windscreen is small and curves back toward the driver.

Rearview mirrors are often mounted on the windscreen if the bike will be driven on the street. Often a fairing made of carbon fiber covers the sides of the bike. The fuel tank sits high, right in front of the driver. The seat is narrow and seats one or two people. The speedometer and tachometer sit above the handlebars.

On the driver's right handlebar is the brake lever, which activates the front wheel brake. The on/off switch and electric start button are also on the right handlebar. The right hand grip is the throttle, and lets the driver control acceleration. On the left handlebar is the clutch lever.

On street legal sport bikes, the horn and turn signal are also on the left side handlebar. The foot pegs sit farther back on sport bikes compared to other bikes. In front of the right foot peg is the brake pedal for the rear wheel.

In front of the left foot peg is the shift pedal, which the driver pushes up and down with his or her foot. First gear is always all the way down. Lifting up the lever puts the bike in neutral, then second, third, fourth, and fifth. Some motorcycles even have six gears.

Sport bikes are built streamlined for speed. Notice how all the edges on the bike are rounded for less resistance.

Parts of the Motorcycle

Most of the motorcycle's parts sit in its chassis. The exhaust pipes aim upwards, so they don't drag on the ground in tight turns. The sound of the exhaust can be very different from bike to bike. Some motorcycles are very quiet, and sound like a purr. Other bikes are very loud and rumble down the road. Most sport bikes are quiet, which is especially typical of Japanese bikes. At high speeds, sport bikes have a high-pitched sound, like a swarm of bees going down the road.

The front forks provide support for the front end of the bike. The fuel tank sits on top of the frame near the front. The seat comes in many different sizes. Sport bikes have a narrow seat, scooped low. Racing bikes don't have room for two people, just enough space for the racer to be comfortable. The engine is positioned between the tires, resting on the frame.

All motorcycles function basically the same way. They are turned on by either an electric push button start or a kick start. Sport bikes have electric starts. Gas and air go into the cylinder. The gas is compressed by a piston and ignited when the spark plug makes a spark. This explosion makes the gas expand, pushing the piston downwards. The crankshaft changes the up and down piston movement into a circular one. The four strokes

of a piston are intake, compression, power, and exhaust. Most sport bikes use four-stroke engines. Two-stroke engines are also sometimes used.

Although the two-stroke engine has less parts and is mechanically simple, its operations are much more complex. Each stroke is doing twice as much as the four-stroke engine. The first stroke is intake and compression, and the second stroke is power and exhaust.

There are many sizes and styles of engines. The fins lining this engine help cool it down when it gets hot.

The transmission system takes the power from the engine and uses it to turn the rear wheel. Most sport bikes are chain driven. Just as on a bicycle, the chain wraps around two sprockets. One sprocket sits in the center of the bike, and one by the rear wheel. If a larger rear and smaller front sprocket is used, top speeds will be slower than if a bigger front and smaller back sprocket is used. The same sprocket principle also holds true on a bicycle.

The chassis, or frame, plays an important role in the handling of the motorcycle. Even 100 years of development hasn't brought any major changes in the principles of chassis design. Motorcycles still have the basic shape of the bicycle. Sport bikes have a low center of gravity, which means that the weight of the chassis and engine sit lower to the ground than other bikes. This makes the bike less top-heavy and easier for the driver to handle. The length of the front forks is important because it effects the stability and cornering of the machine.

Opposite page: Sport bikes are built low to the ground, which gives them a low center of gravity and makes them easier to handle.

Tires

Racing motorcycles usually use racing slicks on days when it's not raining. The smooth, wider surface of the tire allows for the most contact between the tires and the road, which makes the bike faster. Tires with tread are used on rainy days to avoid slipping. Racing tires are wider than regular tires, so drivers have a lot of control going around corners.

The type of tire chosen for a race can make a racer a winner or a loser. Sport bikes that are driven on the road usually have two different sized tires. The front tire is smaller and more narrow. The back tire is larger and wider. This gives the bike a leaned-over, sportier look. It also makes the bike easier to handle and more aerodynamic.

Opposite page: Tires on sport bikes are smooth and wide to grip the road surface while cornering.

Riding Gear

Because a motorcyclist is so vulnerable, special protection gear is needed. Riders need to protect themselves not only in case of an accident, but also against weather conditions. When motorcycles were first invented, riders didn't need a lot of protection simply because their machines didn't go very fast. People wore the same kind of clothes they would while horseback riding or bicycling.

Along with better technology came faster speeds. Today, better protection is needed than it was years ago. A helmet can protect the driver's head in an accident, and also keep the driver warm. Some helmets have visors that keep wind, sun, bugs, and dust out of the driver's face and mouth. Some drivers like the feel of wind on their faces, so they choose a helmet without a visor. Goggles also block out wind and dust from the driver's eyes. Future helmets will have built-in air conditioning.

Racers wear full-coverage helmets with special padding inside to reduce chances of injuries. Racers also wear full body leather suits, with elbow and knee pads. When racers lean into a curve, they use the "knee-down" technique. They slide their knees along the ground for stability, which wears down their knee pads.

A leather jacket can save a driver's skin if he or she is in an accident. Gloves need to be thin enough to allow the driver to operate the controls, but thick enough to be warm. Leather pants or chaps are sometimes worn when the temperature drops. Chaps are leather pant legs that go over regular pants. Someday motorcyclists will be able to buy full body suits that are electronically heated. Cyclists also wear heavy leather boots. The boot toe needs to be thick enough so shifting the foot lever is comfortable.

Motorcyclists have been wearing leather for a long time because it is durable and protects the driver from wind, rain, and road burn in accidents. Over the past decades, the black leather biker jacket has become a symbol of rebellion, and even non-bikers can be seen wearing them.

Safety gear should be worn at all times in case of an accident.

Early Models

The early sport bikes made for street driving didn't look like today's sport bikes. They were made out of steel and chrome. Today's bikes are made of carbon fiber. In 1969, the Honda CB750 came on the market with five speeds, four cylinders, an electric start, and a front disc brake. These features were a first for a street machine. Honda was the only motorcycle manufacturer at that time that could produce a machine like this for an affordable price. In 1970, the CB750 was fine-tuned and put on the race track. It won not only the Daytona 200 Superbike race, but it also captured the consumer market for that year.

Other bikes produced in 1969 weren't as refined as Honda's machine. British manufacturer Norton came out with the Norton Fastback Commando. With a single cylinder 750cc engine, kick start, and drum brakes, the Norton couldn't compete with Honda's new model. In the early 1970s, other manufacturers had time to catch up and started using some of Honda's technology on their bikes.

The Italian-made Ducati built a 750cc Sport in the early 1970s. It had two cylinders and used a single disc brake on the front wheel. In 1973, Kawasaki came out with the Z1. It out-performed Honda's CB750 and became the sport bike of the 1970s.

Older model sport bikes aren't as flashy as some of today's models.

New Models

In the 1980s, almost every manufacturer began making its own version of the sport bike. Japanese manufacturers kept trying to out-do themselves by building bigger and heavier motorcycles. What they didn't do, however, was complement the heavier weight with better handling. Kawasaki's Z1300 is a prime example of this not-so-great heavy bike idea. Suzuki brought new styling to the sport bike. The 1982 Katana looked radical. Its styling is similar to today's Suzukis.

In the 1990s, British, Italian, German, and American motorcycles have kept up with Japanese technology. One of the leaders is the Italian-made Bimota. These hand finished machines are designed to fit engines made by other companies. In 1998, Bimota made their own engines. Around 300 bikes are made each year. Bimota developed a unique steering system. Yamaha is now taking notes from Bimota's technology. Buell, an American made motorcycle, promises that their bike sounds like no other sport bike on the road. Harley-Davidson supports Buell financially and has added some of its own touches to the sport bike.

In 1995, Suzuki made the GSXR 1100. Cyclists race this super quick bike because of its excellent handling and stability. The 1997 Honda CBR 1100XX performs with the best of them.

In the future, motorcycles will perform and handle even better than they do today. Motorcycles in the future will have to pollute less. Manufacturers have built prototypes that run on electricity but none that can go very far in one stretch. In the future, motorcycles will be more aerodynamic and more fuel efficient.

One thing that will never change is the love a motorcyclist has for driving his or her machine. Like their drivers, motorcycles have unique spirits and personalities. The angles and lines of each motorcycle are unique, and the sound that pours out of the pipes cannot be duplicated by any other machine. It seems that a motorcycle carries with it a sense of adventure. Along with that sense of adventure, motorcycles are here to stay.

Today's sport bikes are built to be faster than any other motorcycles in history.

Glossary

Aerodynamic - things designed to cut through the wind with less resistance.

Carburetor - mixes air and fuel into a combustible vapor.

CC (cubic centimeters) - used to measure the size of an engine.

Chain driven - a chain is used to transfer the power from the engine to the rear wheel. Belt-driven drives are the other option.

Chassis - the frame of the bike, made out of steel or carbon fiber.

Clutch - the part that engages the power from the engine to the rear wheel.

Consumer - the person who buys a product.

Crankshaft - the part of the engine that changes the up and down movement of the piston into a circular movement.

Cylinder - the piston chamber of the engine.

Disc brake - a single disc brake that is squeezed to a stop.

Drum brake - an older technology brake that is shaped like a drum.

Fairing - the covers on the sides and front of a motorcycle.

Four/Five speed - the number of gears that a motorcycle has.

Foot pegs - the pegs on which the driver and passenger rest their feet.

Front forks - the front suspension that is shaped like a fork.

Kick start - a way of starting the bike, besides the electric start, by kicking a lever down.

Manufacturer - a company that makes a product in large numbers.

Piston - the part that moves up and down in the shaft of the cylinder.

Racing slicks - tires used by racers that are smooth and wide.

Sprocket - a round disc with teeth around which the chain wraps.

Stability - being stable, not tipsy or jarring.

Swing arm - the part of the frame that the wheel sits in, which also acts as part of the suspension.

Transmission - the system that transfers the power from the engine to the rear wheel.

Twin-cylinder engine - two cylinders.

V-twin engine - two cylinders that sit vertically in a V formation.

Internet Sites

Minibike Central
http://www.geocities.com/MotorCity/7029/mini.html
This page shows pictures of awesome bikes and tells how to make them. It also has plenty of photos of minibikes and minicycles. This site will give you information on where to find minibikes and parts.

Pete's SOLO Disabled Motorcycle Project
http://www.btinternet.com/~chaloner/pete/pete.htm
This website is about a different kind of custom bike. The page is for disabled people who want to ride a motorcycle. See photos of this customized bike, and how it works.

The Dirt Bike Pages
http://www.off-road.com/orcmoto.html
This site has action photos of all kinds of dirt bikes, monthly columns and articles, and product reports. This site has important riding information, too.

Scooter Magazine Online
http://www2.scootermag.it/scooter/
This web site is fully devoted to motorscooters. Technique, developments, new models, tests, track and road trials.

The Motorcycle Database
http://www.motorcycle.informaat.nl/ehome.html
Over 250 motorcycles, their specifications and pictures, and driver experiences from visitors. Pick the model and year of motorcycle you would like to see. Photos and detailed information is included. Lots to see!

Pass It On

Motorcycle Enthusiasts: educate readers around the country by passing on information you've learned about motorcycles. Share your little-known facts and interesting stories. Tell others what your favorite kind of motorcycle is or what your favorite type of riding is. We want to hear from you!
To get posted on the ABDO & Daughters website E-mail us at
"Sports@abdopub.com"
Visit the ABDO Publishing Company website at www.abdopub.com

Index